T0115520

MY FIRST
Gymnastics Class

By Alyssa Satin Capucilli
Photographs by Laura Hanifin

Ready-to-Read

Simon Spotlight
New York   London   Toronto   Sydney   New Delhi

This book was previously published with slightly different text and art.

For Molly Isabelle, our newest tumbler!

—A.S.C.

SIMON SPOTLIGHT
An imprint of Simon & Schuster Children's Publishing Division
1230 Avenue of the Americas, New York, New York 10020
This Simon Spotlight edition June 2016
Text copyright © 2012 by Alyssa Satin Capucilli
Photographs and illustrations copyright © 2012 by Simon & Schuster, Inc.
All rights reserved, including the right of reproduction in whole or in part in any form.
SIMON SPOTLIGHT, READY-TO-READ, and colophon are registered trademarks of Simon & Schuster, Inc.
For information about special discounts for bulk purchases, please contact Simon & Schuster Special Sales at
1-866-506-1949 or business@simonandschuster.com.
Manufactured in the United States of America 0816 LAK
2   4   6   8   10   9   7   5   3
Library of Congress Cataloging-in-Publication Data
Names: Capucilli, Alyssa Satin, 1957–
Title: My first gymnastics class / by Alyssa Satin Capucilli ; photographs by Laura Hanifin.
Description: This Simon Spotlight hardcover/paperback edition. | New York : Simon Spotlight, [2016] |
©2012. | Series: Ready-to-Read | Audience: Ages: 3–5.
Identifiers: LCCN 2016003218 | ISBN 9781481461870 (paperback : alk. paper) |
ISBN 9781481461894 (hardcover : alk. paper) | ISBN 9781481461900 (eBook)
Subjects: LCSH: Gymnastics for children—Juvenile literature.
Classification: LCC GV464.5 .C33 2016 | DDC 796.44083—dc23
LC record available at http://lccn.loc.gov/2016003218
This book was previously published with slightly different text and art.

It is my very first gymnastics class!

This leotard is
just right for me.

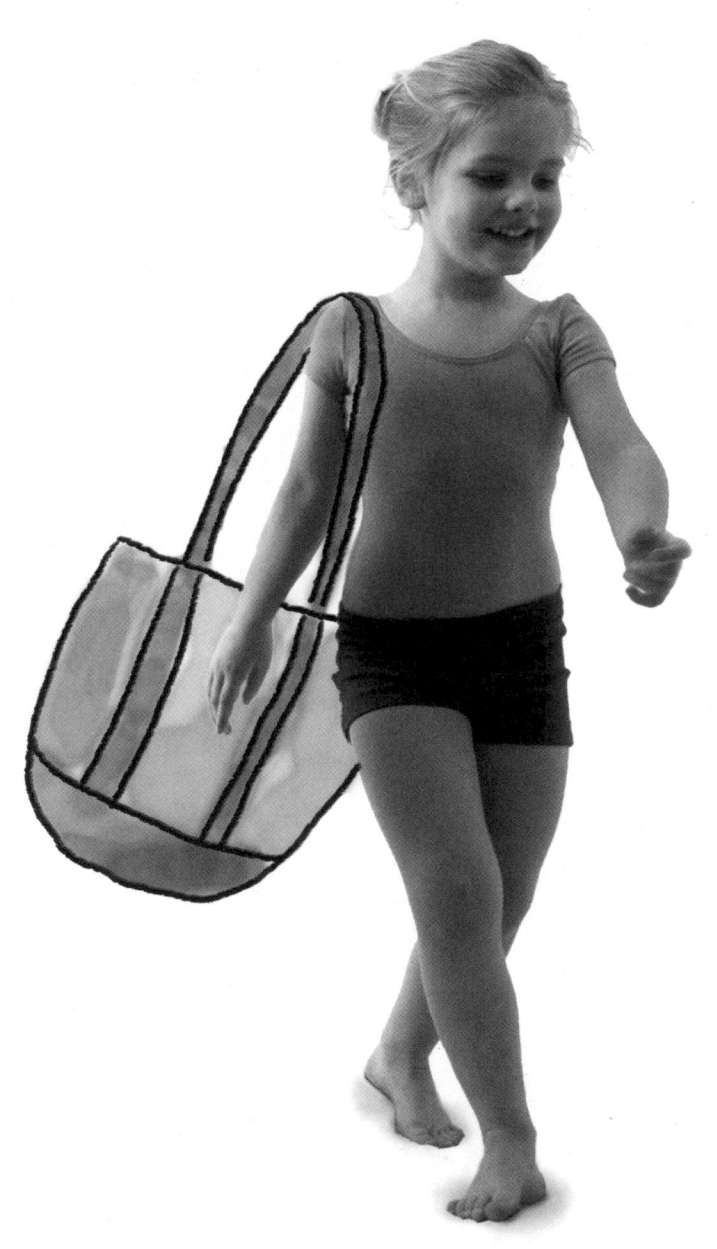

Now that I am ready to go,
I wonder what I will see.

We stand on the mat, straight and tall.

Then we jump and
stretch our arms wide.

We warm up our bodies as we touch our toes.

We bend and reach
to each side!

We learn a pike.

We learn a tuck.

We learn a straddle, too.

"It takes practice," Coach Rose says.

There are so many things
we can do!

We can leap like frogs.

We can spin like logs.

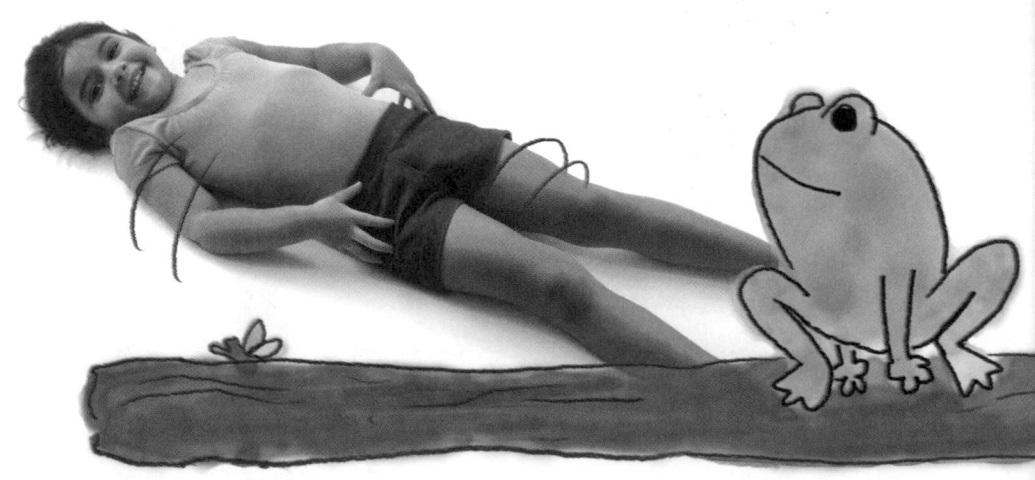

We can hop just like kangaroos!

We can walk like a

tightrope walker.

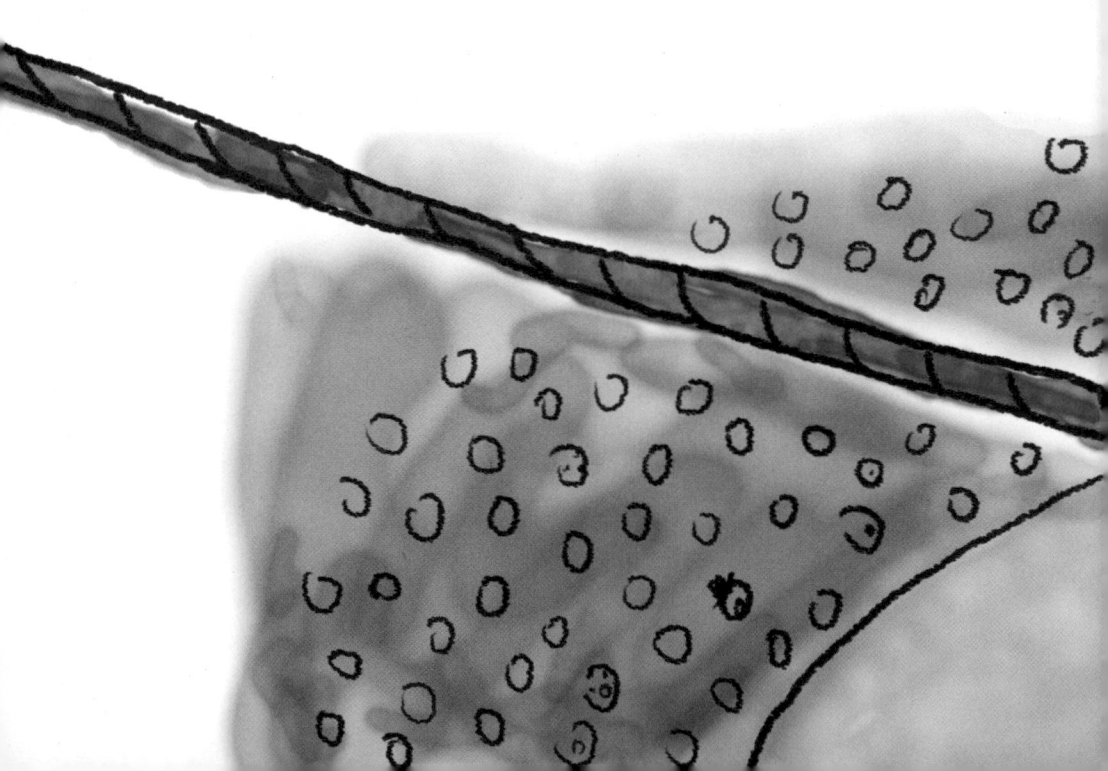

We balance just like they do!

Hands up high.

Head down low.

I can roll like a ball.

Off I go!

Soon I will be ready to jump, swing, and climb!

Gymnastics is fun!
I had a great time!

Do you want to be a gymnast?

Don't forget to find a grown-up to

help you read and learn about the

gymnastics moves in this book!

Warm up!

1 Stand Tall

Stand straight and tall on your mat or a soft surface. Keep your feet together and arms at your side. You look like the letter **I**!

Now jump! Open your legs and arms wide. Now you look like a big letter **X**!

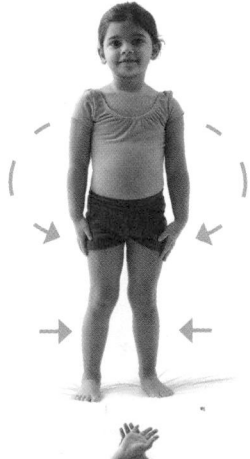

2 Jump and Stretch

Jump again and close your arms and legs.

Jump wide and clap your hands over your head. Get your muscles nice and warm.

3
Touch Your Toes

Start with your legs wide. See the
triangle between your legs?

Can you touch your toes?

First try to touch one foot and then the other.
No tickling now!